Spots

by Heather Gray

HOUGHTON MIFFLIN HARCOURT
School Publishers

PHOTOGRAPHY CREDITS: Cover © Digital Vision/Getty Images; 1 © Artville; 2 © Artville; 3 © 1996 PhotoDisc, Inc.; 4 © Digital Vision/Getty Images; 5 © Pixland/Corbis; 6 © Nico Smit/Alamy; 7 © 1996 PhotoDisc, Inc.; 8 © 1997 PhotoDisc, Inc./Alan D. Carey; 9 © Getty; 10 © Tom Grill/Corbis

Printed in China

ISBN-13: 978-0-547-42729-4
ISBN-10: 0-547-42729-8

10 11 12 13 0940 18 17 16 15 14 13
4500443494

The dog has brown spots.
The spots never come off.

The cat has its own spots.

The frog has spots.
You know what color
the spots are.

The fish has spots.
You know what color
the spots are.

The bird has spots.

The spots are very small.

The cow has spots.
The spots are very big.

The horse has spots.
The spots are brown.

The bug has spots.
The spots are black.

The girl has spots.
She has been out
in the sun.

Responding

WORDS TO KNOW **Word Builder**

Name something that is brown.

Talk About It

Text to World What animals are brown?

✔ WORDS TO KNOW

been	**off**
brown	**out**
know	**own**
never	**very**

✔ **TARGET STRATEGY** Question

Ask questions about what you are reading.